Birds of San Pancho
and Other Poems of Place

Also by Lucille Lang Day

POETRY
Becoming an Ancestor
The Curvature of Blue
Infinities
Wild One
Fire in the Garden
Self-Portrait with Hand Microscope

POETRY CHAPBOOKS
Dreaming of Sunflowers: Museum Poems
God of the Jellyfish
The Book of Answers
Lucille Lang Day: Greatest Hits, 1975–2000

MEMOIR
Married at Fourteen: A True Story

CHILDREN'S BOOKS
The Rainbow Zoo
Chain Letter

ANTHOLOGIES EDITED
Fire and Rain: Ecopoetry of California (with Ruth Nolan)
Red Indian Road West: Native American Poetry from California
(with Kurt Schweigman)

SCIENCE EDUCATION
*How to Encourage Girls in Math and Science: Strategies for
Parents and Educators* (with Joan Skolnick and Carol Langbort)

*SEEK (Science Exploration, Excitement, and Knowledge):
A Curriculum in Health and Biomedical Science
for Diverse 4th and 5th Grade Students* (editor)

Family Health and Science Festival: A SEEK Event (editor)

Birds of San Pancho
and Other Poems of Place

Lucille Lang Day

BLUE LIGHT PRESS ◆ 1ST WORLD PUBLISHING

SAN FRANCISCO ◆ FAIRFIELD ◆ DELHI

Birds of San Pancho and Other Poems of Place

Copyright ©2020, Lucille Lang Day

BLUE LIGHT PRESS
www.bluelightpress.com
bluelightpress@aol.com

1ST WORLD PUBLISHING
PO Box 2211
Fairfield, IA 52556
www.1stworldpublishing.com

BOOK & COVER DESIGN
Melanie Gendron
melaniegendron999@gmail.com

COVER PHOTOGRAPH: Great Kiskadee
Luis E. Morales-Vallín, Director
San Pancho Birding Network
www.birdingsanpancho.net

AUTHOR PHOTO
Hilary Brodey

FIRST EDITION

Library of Congress Control Number: 2020941068

ISBN: 9781421836645

For Richard

Contents

I. Foreigner

II. Between the Two Shining Seas

I
Foreigner

It Matters

San Miguel de Allende, Mexico

that the casa rises,
orange as the dawn sky
under cloud and blue,

impatiens—white, red, pink—
spilling from terracotta pots
along the balustrade;

that feathery jacaranda leaves flutter
and the bells of La Parroquia wake us
at six a.m. each morning;

that the gnarled woman begging
on the street was once young and agile
and that someone give her

a few pesos when she reaches out
from the sidewalk by the bank
in the sticky heat of late afternoon;

that even here I remember
my father's laugh and the weight
of my mother's disappointments,

while *les étoiles*, *las estrellas*, the stars
burn through the sky's dark cloth
no matter what I call them;

that prickly pear cacti are delicious
although the Big Bang defies
common sense and intuition,

and earth and sea offer their riches
freely to the boy playing
with a stick outside La Casa Rosada;

that he never have to hold a gun
and the bells always reach his ears,
pulsing through clear morning air.

Roses

San Miguel de Allende, Mexico

No need to write about
the dozen peach-colored roses
in a transparent vase
on a chest of drawers
sitting on a red tile floor
in a bright green room in Mexico.

They appeared yesterday—
a gift, but not meant
especially for me.
I looked into the window
of the room next door
and saw twelve orchid-pink ones.

Still, a gift is a gift, so I
will accept their sweet breath
as firecrackers announce
la Natividad de San Juan Bautista,
fiesta music rises,
and night's dark petals fall.

Fiesta

San Miguel de Allende, Mexico

All the stars switch on above the street
as fiesta music rises from the square.
Girls in sequined blue jeans tap their feet,
and jacarandas shimmy in the air.
Accordions, guitars, and trumpets sing
for people swaying on the cobblestones
in yellow, red, and blue embroidered clothing
and skeletons who shake their graceful bones.

But I will always be a stranger here
where roosters crow and church bells ring at dawn.
The language comes like birdcalls to my ear;
I want to dance, but I won't be here long
enough to learn the steps or even know
when the dead stop jigging where they go.

Birds of San Pancho
Nayarit, Mexico

A great kiskadee sits on the casa wall
belting its exuberant song above
the dusty cobblestone street. The bird
is masked like a raccoon, its breast
yellow as the butterflies that flit
amid hibiscus and bougainvillea.

Far from the casa, where palms
and Maya nut trees grow lushly,
a yellow-winged cacique waits
in the paperbark tree, the lemony
underside of its long tail cascading
like silk. It surveys the scene, ignoring
the golden-cheeked woodpecker,
streak-backed oriole, flycatchers
and scrub euphonia sharing the *selva*.

Farther down the dirt road, where
red ants live inside acacia thorns,
a pale cow wanders alone, snubbing
the fat chachalacas singing *chachalaca*
as I pass by. It seems the birds are out
to cheer me, though I know food
and mates are what they're after.
A whole flock of orange-fronted
parakeets feasts on berries overhead.

Later, at the lagoon, a great blue heron,
a little blue heron, a green heron,
a night heron, two great egrets, eight
snowy egrets and twenty cattle egrets

gather while brown pelicans dive
for fish and the sun's bright disk sinks
into the sea. When it disappears,
the egrets rise in groups and pairs
to settle in two coconut palms
for the night. Oh, to sit up there too—
safe, having eaten my fill—with
folded wings, watching over creation.

Hologram

In my dream, my daughter shimmered
on stage as a hologram, giving a lecture
on sexual dysfunction for her fellow
marriage and family therapists. They
nodded and laughed at all the right times.

I wanted to tell them she was such
a terrific speaker, so witty and animated,
because she'd studied dramatic art.
I knew that she knew she had cancer
but expected to live. Only I knew
she was already dead. No way
would I tell her and break her heart.

She was still my baby who'd bounced
in time to the music of the Beatles,
my mischievous toddler, my girl
who sang on stage at Fairyland at five.

Waking to the sea's murmur at Casa
Obelisco in San Pancho, Mexico,
in my room with the cool tile floor
and a fan turning slowly overhead,
I understood: this was what had happened.

Through all the long months of chemo—
R-CHOP, RICE, R-DHAP, GEMOX—
PET scans and radiation treatments,
both of us snubbed death—the hated
stranger grinning smugly, waiting so near.

Even as the tissues around her lungs
filled with fluid from the tumor
and her breathing grew labored, I held
her hand and told her, over and over,
*Hang onto hope, Liana. You can still
get better,* as though my love could
scratch a diamond or hold back the night.

Resplendent Quetzals

Monteverde Cloud Forest, Costa Rica

Male and female, they sit like gods, high
in an aguacatillo tree, surveying the forest:

small black fruits they will eat from red cups
fig trees strangling the trumpet trees that host them

green vipers with yellow stripes, nearly invisible
where they knot themselves around branches

lancebill hummingbirds dipping in light
violet sabrewings visiting red blooms of the shrimp plant

cardio orchids that pulse like the hearts of small birds
tarantulas dozing in nests in holes in the forest floor

woodcreepers pecking for insects on trunks
mottled owls asleep in the canopy

black-faced solitaires emitting their squeaky-gate call
humans and the mosquitoes that feast on them.

The quetzals see it all and know it is good.
The male puffs his bright red chest,

adjusts his flowing blue-green cloak. Mist settles,
making his feathers and all the leaves of the cloud forest shine.

His lady watches, dazzled, but these gods cannot rest.
Every year there will be a nest and young to hatch:
so much remains to be created.

Birthday Gifts from the Rainforest
Arenal, Costa Rica

A howler monkey dining in a cecropia tree
A trogon dressed in yellow, blue and green
His dowdier mate
The blood tree oozing red sap

A river of leaf-cutter ants carrying bits of leaves,
much bigger than their bodies, to their nest
Antbirds and wrens
chattering and flapping

A pygmy squirrel hunched on a branch
Heliconias with leaves like orange beaks
Sleepy hibiscus whose pistils stick out
from pink buds that never open

Whiptail lizards rushing
every which way across the path
Rattlesnake plants shaking spiky yellow
blossom stalks like beads

A baby viper curled on a leaf
Monkey tail ferns and elephant ear plants
Rufous-tailed hummingbirds savoring
purple blossoms of porterweed

A palm whose above-ground roots
look like huge penises
All the creatures looking down at me, twice
as old as I'd like to be, but not yet done with wonder

The Real Thing

Palo Verde National Park, Costa Rica

In a boat skimming past red and black
mangroves, close-packed, leaning
over the briny Rio Tempisque,
where crocodiles swim, the scales
down the middle of their backs
breaking the water's murky surface
like chains of floating rocks, I think
of the Jungle Cruise in Disneyland,
my father beside me when I was eight.
When the fake crocodile opened
its jaws, he said, "How would you like
to see the real thing?" I said I would
and meant it but knew I'd never go
with him. He feared planes, boats
and the depth of rivers, but now
I'm looking into the eyes of a live
crocodile in a jungle river: pale
green marbles, the pupils vertical
black slits. The crocodile regards me
with no apparent interest while herons
dip for fish, iguanas bask on branches
overhead, and roseate spoonbills
splash the sky with pink. Howler
monkeys stay high in the trees, but
white-faced capuchins crowd around
the boat when we stop. One climbs on
the roof. Another poops from a limb
a few feet away. It hits the water
with a splash. Daddy, who put
so many ideas in my head, I hope
you're looking down from heaven
at this monkey relieving itself
beside me, then popping a big black
spider into its mouth: it's the real thing.

Time on Rábida

Galápagos Islands

On Rábida, where the sand is red,
three white-cheeked pintails
swam in a brackish lagoon
beneath a ruddy hill
of basaltic rock formed
when magma from an ancient
volcano cooled in the sea.
It didn't matter what time
it was when I was there,
what day, or even what year.
Yesterday, today and tomorrow
were all the same to the finches.
Passing saltbush, prickly pear
cacti and leafless incense trees
adorned with tufts of moss,
I spotted a marine iguana
lounging near an outcropping
of rock where a lone cactus
grew high above the waves,
and somewhere on the path
I lost my watch with the brown
leather band and round face
encircled by rhinestones.
I was happy to be timeless
like the warblers and flycatchers
and wondered if a bird might
find my watch and use it
to decorate its nest, but then
someone found it and gave it
back to me with a broken band,
and I looked at it sadly, longing
for wings, a swift escape.

What the Tortoises Know

Galápagos Islands

On Genovesa, as my husband lay
on the beach of Darwin Bay,
a sea lion came to sniff his toes
and a red-footed booby, sitting
with her chick in a mangrove
nearby, let me get kissing-close.

On North Seymour, the frigate birds
weren't fazed by me, and a young
blue-footed booby was intrigued
by my walking stick. On Española,
the sand was so thick with iguanas,
it was hard not to step on them.

The guide explained that the animals
here don't fear us, hawks and short-
eared owls being the only predators
evolution has bred them to know.
They first saw humans with guns
and bows just five hundred years ago.

But giant tortoises, who live to be one
hundred fifty years old, have seen
how we kill to make boxes and combs,
so heads and legs withdraw into shells
at the sound of a loud voice and
they grow still as clean-picked bones.

Inauguration Day in the Galápagos
January 20, 2017

The forecast that morning said possible rain,
but the air was dry, the sky cloudy,
as our bus climbed the hill on Santa Cruz,
taking us to the Tortoise Ecological Reserve
at the top of the island. We passed corn,
sugar cane and coffee plantations, stands
of cedars, and ranches where scrawny
cattle grazed. At the Reserve we borrowed
clumsy rubber boots to lumber through
the muddy terrain where giant tortoises,
like smooth, ancient dome-shaped rocks,
munched on low-lying plants. We hiked
through a lava tube on our way back
to the visitor center, where small brown
finches hopped and flitted about the tables.
No one mentioned the inauguration.

In the afternoon, our ship headed for Plaza Sur,
and as we waited for zodiacs to take us
to the island, the Mormon Tabernacle Choir
was singing, prelude to a second showing
of the inauguration. My turn to debark
came quickly and I saw dark marine iguanas
and golden land ones basking side by side.
Sea lions played in the waves. A yellow
warbler perched on a shrub; a short-eared
owl hid beneath it. Red carpetweed
dotted with prickly pear cacti spread in all
directions. Flocks of shearwaters and petrels
flashed beneath cliffs as frigate birds
dove for fish. Back on the ship, I was later

told, a man had threatened to jump overboard
if they showed the inauguration again,
so they waited until he was safe on Plaza Sur
surrounded by iguanas, others charmed
by blue-footed boobies, and the insistent
surge of the imperiled, luminous sea.

Global Warming in the Galápagos

Three years without rain,
and incense trees are gray, leafless
in what should be the wet season.

Without the trees, where will red-
footed boobies with blue beaks
build nests where fluffy chicks can hatch?

Even prickly pear cacti, looking so much
like clusters of spiny ping pong paddles,
are turning brown and dying.

What will happen to iguanas that eat
the cacti, and lava lizards that nibble
lice from the iguanas' necks and backs?

A warming sea also brings El Niño
with too much rain, flooding,
overheated currents where penguins

can't find fish, and beaches so hot
that green turtle eggs can't hatch.
When iguanas can no longer regulate

their body temperature, giant tortoises
and blue-footed boobies will gather
like refugees and strike out for cooler land.

On the Aegean

Rosy-fingered dawn reaches over silhouetted hillsides
studded with scrubby oaks. Cypress spires point
toward the sky above cliffs that drop abruptly
to the amoeboid coast whose pseudopods
of land project into the sea as villages
on the shoreline wink and glitter.

We stop on dry, rocky islands
where windmills keep turning on hills
with white stone houses on narrow, winding streets.
Vineyards grow without irrigation, vines close to earth
in constant wind. The grapes will be stomped
by foot, then goats will clear weeds.

The sea is turquoise close to shore,
dark blue farther out where the water
is deeper. Between islands, the sea leaps
and churns. It undulates, ever-changing in shape
and color. Seven-foot swells, crowned with foam,
look twice that high. I watch, amazed, from a porthole.

I'm not seasick, but wonder if I should be afraid
on this sailing ship so far from land. No—
people crossed this way thousands
of years ago, refugees today
cling to boats that leak. I close
my eyes; the sea rocks me to sleep.

Yom Kippur in Ephesus and Patmos

Eve

In front of the two-story façade
of the Library of Celsus,
third largest in the ancient
world with its 12,000 scrolls,
near the broad street where
Mark Antony and Cleopatra
strolled and fell in love, I dine
at dusk on dolma, hummus,
veal, rice and chocolate mousse
when I should be fasting.
The Apostle Paul preached
at the theater here and so did
John the Evangelist. Angered
by John's claims of miracles
and eternal life, the Roman
Emperor exiled him to Patmos.

Morning

On a hillside of Patmos
above a bay surrounded
by brown slopes and white
stone houses, I visit the cave
where John, the youngest
apostle, wrote his Gospel
and the Book of Revelation,
both said to have been
dictated by Jesus to John
and by John to his scribe.
I duck under the rock

that split into three parts
to signify father, son and holy
ghost. There's a monastery
built around the cave, but
only two monks remain,
chanting morning prayers
on the Day of Atonement.

Afternoon

A shopkeeper in a boutique
farther up the hill on Patmos
says, "You're Jewish,
aren't you?" when I ask
the price of a scarf. I say
yes, and the plump woman
says, "I know you people.
I've been to Brooklyn."
A nonobservant convert
from California, shopping
on Yom Kippur but still
hoping forgiveness might
be arranged, I wonder where
the scarves were made—
India or Athens—and how
we recognize love or hate
in a stranger's face.

Dining Alone in Athens

Strofi restaurant

On a rooftop beneath the Acropolis, I have
sea bass wrapped in vine leaves, served
with white wine sauce and olives. Yes,
a true feast! The Erechtheion and Parthenon
rise above me, columns lit and glowing against
the darkening sky. Though cracked and crumbling
after twenty-five hundred years, they're more
intact than the Arch of Hadrian and once
towering Temple of Zeus on a field below.
Athena planted the first olive tree here
in a contest against Poseidon, whose magic
was seawater. The twelve gods of Olympus
declared her the winner and gave the city
her name. But now the old gods are gone,
their statues in museums, their temples in ruins.
Around me, parties of men in short-sleeved shirts
and women in sleeveless white dresses chatter;
couples gaze at each other, speaking softly.
I order baklava to share with my husband, age
seventy-six, who waits, neither sick nor well,
back in our hotel room, and I complain
to the moon that even the gods are fleeting,
but I like that story. The tree. The goddess
who holds her own against the sea.

Reverie Interrupted

Mauve blinds quiver on a bedroom window
in Paris, green metal shutters folded back.
Five stories down, in the courtyard
an old well rises like a stone tub
surrounded with pink and lilac flowers.

Under neighbors' windows
red and orange ones spill raucously
from planters, clouds drifting
behind the tile roof. A blue tit lands
on a dormer, and I wonder
about the meaning of each moment
and how to hold it the way
Monet and van Gogh
caught haystacks and orchards
in particular seasons and light.

Surely each moment is worth preserving,
I think as I hear a sudden banging—
Betsy, back from class, fumbling
with a stuck lock, and I know
that this moment, distinct
from all others, is the one
when I must rise to let her in.

Foreigner

The women here wear tight pants,
stylish boots and cute jackets.
In my walking shoes, baggy khakis
and Eddie Bauer hoodie, I am
an obvious foreigner, *une Americaine
à Paris*. When I catch a man staring
at me in the Champs de Mars
Métro station, I doubt he's admiring
my beauty. More likely, he's noting
that I am anxious and disoriented,
a good target for a pickpocket.
Perhaps he is one, like the guy
who got my coin purse and keys
years ago at the Saint-Paul station
or the one who snatched my money
and makeup bag in Dublin while
I studied a map. A woman's
voice announces in English
over the paging system: *There is
a pickpocket in the station. Watch
your purse and wallet.* I clutch
my purse more tightly, change
trains at Neuilly-Porte Maillot,
make it back to Jean's apartment
in the Marais, where I've left
my passport and check register
with all the passwords to access
my credit card accounts online.
The check register is missing.
Searching my luggage again
and again, I try to concentrate

on Chagall's bride and groom
flying over the city, the view
of Notre Dame from a cloud,
myself an invisible dot somewhere
down there, needing to descend
the four flights of tilted stairs,
walk past the old well festooned
with flowers, find a bistro with
a little round table out front,
and order duck paté with a glass
of Sancerre, or a crisp Vouvray.

Evenk Shaman's Costume

musée du quai Branly, Paris

In a glass case, temperature
and light kept low, the headdress
with metal antlers is still,
but the nineteenth-century shaman
who wore it leapt like a reindeer buck
to defend himself among spirits.

.

The long fringes of his dress swayed
when he stamped with drum and baton
to cure madness, disease and pain.
Let there be magic! A dance
in a sacred grove, to cast evil spirits
from bodies, retrieve stolen souls.

His sleeves billow and stiffen
into wings as he flies over oceans
with spirits of fish and water birds
clanging on his back, noisier
than the families who shuffle
past his costume now and point.

Water Lilies

Giverny, France

Pink and yellow, they float
on pads in clusters
forming blue-green mats

Yes, I have entered the painting
to stand on the Japanese bridge
framed by bamboo

a weeping willow
and hanging wisteria, all reflected
in water that's nearly still

The bland gray sky
doesn't matter
nor does my internal weather

Near the pink house
irises are out
in white and purple ruffles

Poppies swish red skirts
like flamenco dancers
I must remember how they sway

Inside, the dining room is yellow
as an egg yolk
the blue-and-white tiled kitchen

lined with copper pots
Japanese prints adorn walls
in almost every room

Like moments repeating in memory
Hokusai's wave rolls forever
its promise unchanged

TGV, Paris to Arles

Green and yellow fields rush by
swiftly as a lifetime
or a nocturne by Chopin,
whose grave at Père Lachaise Cemetery
is still decked with fresh
red and white roses, one hundred
sixty years after his death.
Jim Morrison rests nearby,
quiet as the sky over that hill
crowded with crypts.

White cows and goats drowse in pastures
and vineyards stretch into the distance
while I eat falafel, packed
last night on rue des Rosiers,
and wonder about the lives
tucked into houses
with orange tile roofs, appearing,
then vanishing again
like forgotten tunes.

Each life so much like mine:
not public like the Jardin
du Luxembourg, or expansive
as the Louvre, but specific
as a silver train headed
toward Roman ruins
on a spring morning, filled
with people eating breakfast,
recalling medieval streets,
graves, blue moons.

Vincent's Bedroom in Arles

The upstairs room in the yellow house
across the street from the Roman arena
in Arles is almost as he painted it: bowl
and pitcher on a small table, two chairs,
a bed with yellow sheets and a red comforter,
the only difference a second small table
with a box for the artist's brushes and palette.
For a few euros, you can enter this fiction.
The actual corner house that Vincent rented
from Widow Venissac in 1888 was hit
by an Allied bomb, blown into history.

But who can say what's real? The same
Provençal sun warms this house as the one
where he wanted to fill his guest room
with paintings of sunflowers. "I want
to make it into a true artist's house," he wrote.
"Everything—from the chairs to the pictures—
should have character." And if this character
is captured by designers who copied his room
here on a street where he must have walked,
perhaps this is now a true artist's house too,
where one could go mad dreaming of sunflowers.

Abandoned in Sarlat

My husband drove away, leaving me
on Boulevard Eugène la Roy
in Sarlat, France, on a May morning,
near the Hotel Madeleine with its blue
shutters and saffron stones. I wondered
if I'd taken too long in the bathroom
that morning, or made too much noise
typing on my computer the night before.

Walking around the corner to Rue
de la République, I didn't have the heart
to browse at La Lune Enchantée with
its figurines, masks and little jewelry
boxes in the window, the L'Oie Blanche
with brightly colored scarves out front,
or even Maison Pélégris, which boasted
selling *magret de canard gras* since 1890.

Trying not to panic, I contemplated
the monument inscribed *Aux Enfants
de Sarlat Morts Pour la Patrie*, 1914
to 1918, and the one that said *Aux Heros
de la Liberation de l'Arrondissement
de Sarlat*, 1940 to 1945, which stood
behind a fountain surrounded by grass
and yellow, white and orange flowers.

Later my husband said he'd spotted
a parking place but couldn't fit
our rental car into it. Then he got lost,
couldn't find his way back to me

or even to our B&B, Le Jardin. Still
I wept, remembering that men and boys
died in those wars and women waited,
whose husbands never returned.

Artists at Chauvet

To reach the entrance they plunged
through underbrush and followed
a narrow path obstructed by rocks
and brambles. Once inside they lit
lamps that burned animal fat
to illuminate ceilings and walls.
In a funnel-shaped room where
huge, elklike creatures roamed
on the walls, they built a hearth
to make charcoal, then painted
and carved overlapping animals,
perhaps to show movement or depth.
In one passage they drew four horses,
carefully scraping the stone smooth
beneath each throat. The fourth horse,
outlined in charcoal and filled
with brown, has a dark black line
at the corner of the lips, creating
an expression of surprise. The artist
must have been surprised himself
by its perfection. Recalling it
as he looked down later at the river
and the valley dotted with pines,
he knew his father and mother
had died, his wife would die,
he would die, and their children
would die, but his astonished horse—
galloping through the cave past
stalagmites and stalactites with bison,
aurochs and rhinos—would survive.

Child's Grave and Finery

A ten-thousand-year-old grave
of a child about three years old,
covered with ochre dust
and marked with three stones,
nestled in a rock shelter
under an overhanging cliff
in southern France. More
than fifteen hundred beads,
carefully carved from seashells
and animal teeth, adorned his neck,
wrists, elbows, ankles and knees.

Marks inside the beads show
a needle passed through them:
they were sewn onto clothes
that disintegrated long ago.
Scratches and nicks on the outside
imply the child wore these beaded
clothes when he was playing.

Anthropologists say this finery
must signify hereditary social status.
But maybe he was an only child
whose grandmother polished
the beads and sewed them
onto his clothes while his father
hunted and his mother gathered
berries, the way a grandmother
today might knit or crochet
a sweater or blanket. Or maybe
his parents were so broken

by his death that they sewed
all their own beads onto
his burial clothes, so anyone
finding his grave would know
how much he mattered.

The Empire of Lights

After a painting by René Magritte,
Royal Museums of Fine Arts of Belgium

The daytime sky does not
    illuminate trees
or the green-shuttered house
    reflected in water.

An old-fashioned streetlamp
    gleams against gloom.
It's day and night at the same time,
    summer and winter

in a place where I am both
    a child riding a merry-go-round
and a solitary adult
    gazing at a painting.

Lights come on in two windows.
    Is dawn breaking?
Or is it still night
    under clouds that float

in a commonplace blue sky
    holding back its brightness?

Pygmalion

After a painting by Paul Delvaux,
Royal Museums of Fine Arts of Belgium

I adore him, though he's gray and cold,
carved in marble, armless and legless.
I wrap my own arms around his neck
and press my nakedness against his torso.

On the ground our shadows embrace
on a field of stones in front of a hillside
where little or nothing grows. Another
naked woman takes a stroll behind me.

A plant sprouts from her head; a flower
floats before her. She is abundance,
a garden. A man in a black hat and coat
hurries by the way men do, doesn't notice.

At least my own man doesn't disappear.
When he wakes, we'll drink Cabernet,
walk down the Champs-Elysées. I snuggle
closer, whisper in his ear; I think he hears.

Dinner in Barcelona
Café de l'Accademia

A dish of small green olives, tart
and salty; a basket of bread; two
cups of soup, pink gazpacho
and creamy carrot vichyssoise;
salad of mixed greens, asparagus,
tomato, tuna and egg; a glass
of Spanish white wine; salmon
stuffed with cheese for Richard,
cod with tapenade for me, all
served at a dimly lit restaurant
while young men shoot glowing
disks toward the sickle moon
hanging over the cathedral plaza
where a band played till midnight
on Saturday and white-shoed
dancers did a slow circle dance
to celebrate Catalan freedom
on Sunday at noon. For now
nothing matters except that
the salmon and cod are perfectly
cooked, the wine is chilled, I've
recovered from my stomach illness,
Gaudi's pillars branch like trees
in La Sagrada Familia, Miro's
moons and stars hang in many-
colored firmaments, and guitar
music rises toward the ceramic
roses on the Palau's ceiling,
each note luscious, true.

The Lark's Wing, Encircled with Golden Blue, Rejoins the Heart of the Poppy Sleeping on the Diamond-Studded Meadow

After a painting at Fundació Joan Miró, Barcelona

The lark's wing: a black oval
floating, buoyed by
a patch of blue sky
small as an inner tube
in the sun's yellow pool

A black band separates
earth from sky below,
the poppy's heart a red dot
beating on a meadow

On another wall
a woman combs her hair
while a little girl skips
past a moon and star

Let the woman skip
with the girl to a place
where the moon sails free
Let the girl find a planet
where stars grow on trees

as my feet rejoin the earth
where the heart
of the poppy sleeps

Last Day in Amsterdam

We make love in our room with fifteen-foot ceilings
and a vinyl Rembrandt behind the bed,
then lunch on leftover sandwiches.
Afterward we buy fusidic acid for pink eye
at the *apotheek* on the corner
and almond cookies at a bakery nearby.

Walking to the Hermitage in chilly May wind
while dappled sunlight pokes
through clouds hanging in low bunches
as they often do here, I keep
my hands deep in my pockets
so my fingertips won't turn white.

The canals—lined with black, red, pink, gray,
brown, and beige brick houses—
glitter everywhere the thin light strikes them.
The paintings at the Hermitage
are by Rubens, van Dyck, Jordaens, and Teniers.
Dancing peasants, witches cooking, and wilted tulips
please me more than biblical figures,
kings and queens, and all the dead fish.

Tomorrow we'll board a train to Paris.
Thin-blade modern windmills—
enough propellers to lift the whole country—
will be turning. Sliced
by irrigation channels, the flat
green landscape will quickly slip by.

I'll remember dodging bicycles
outside the Mellow Yellow Coffeeshop
with its hookah in the window, climbing
steep stairs to the small dark rooms
of Anne Frank's secret annex, and watching
women in bright bikinis with jewels in their navels
beckon from red-light windows while
talking on their cell phones and smiling, maybe
feeling sorry for all the dowdy women in blue jeans
who also do it every day, but don't get paid.

Clichés from the Caves

Orvieto, Italy

Grind

It was a grind at the old grind
where four donkeys were chained
to the grindstone all day
in a high-ceilinged Etruscan cave
enlarged in the Middle Ages.
They walked in a circle, turning
the heavy stone to crush olives
into oil to be served with bread
baked golden brown as the fields
in autumn, mozzarella, and ripe
tomatoes that tasted of the sun.

Pigeons

The pigeons were pigeonholed
in row upon row of pigeonholes
carved in volcanic rock. The grid
of holes went from floor to ceiling
in caves under the town. Two eggs
every twenty-eight days from each
female pigeon ensured a supply
of birds to be plucked and gutted,
washed in red wine, sprinkled
with sea salt and pepper, then
cooked till their juices gleamed.

Well

All's well that ends well, so long
as no one falls in the well
in the cave, dug more than

two thousand years ago by men
who went up and down it, putting
their feet in holes they'd chiseled
in stone like mountain climbers
today, so there would be water
for warm baths, the potters
at their wheels, and people feasting
on sweet tomatoes and pigeon pie.

Fountain

Twice in a lifetime I've walked
down narrow, cobblestone streets
to the Trevi Fountain, where Neptune stands
between two Tritons, one struggling
with a wild horse of the sea, the other leading
a tame one. The first time I was on a tour.
Pierre, the obnoxious guide, said throw
one coin in to get married, two
to get divorced, three to return to Rome,
but I had no coins in my purse or pocket.
Still, in the thirty-three years since,
I've gotten married, gotten divorced,
and returned to Rome. This time,
with my third husband, I've brought
three coins to toss, ensuring another visit.
I reach back, then fling my arm forward
and let go as young men clamor around us,
selling roses and offering to take our picture.
Later, I read the legend of the fountain,
learn Pierre got it wrong: it's one coin
to return to Rome, two to find
a new love, or three to get married
or divorced. What have I done?
I don't want to get married or divorced.
I just want to press my fingers into his flesh
and let his lips cover mine until joy
rises and bursts into light, like water
spilling from a fountain in Rome.

Almost Mugged in Lucca

It was the day I hiked all the way
around the city, the same day we saw
the Tomb of Ilaria, who married the Lord
of Lucca when she was twenty-four,
in 1405, and died two years later
after the birth of her second child.

Her marble sarcophagus, fit
for a pharaoh, has cherubs around
the base and a sculpture of Ilaria
sleeping on top in an elegant gown
and a hat with flowers, a little dog
curled at her feet, her nose worn down

by generations of young women
who rubbed it for luck in love. *Luck?*
We'd just had dinner at Locanda
di Bucco—gazpacho, shrimp
with rice, beef ravioli—and walked
a few blocks to see the oval plaza

that had once been a Roman
amphitheater, when three men, young,
large, emerged from the shadows
and came toward us. They followed
us to a closed store where we stopped
to admire purses in the window.

Quiet as owls listening for mice,
they surrounded us. "I don't like this,"
I said. We headed quickly to the next
block, where people were strolling
and a police car was parked, as the men
disappeared into a pocket of the night.

Buon Giorno

My first time in Europe, a curly-haired
young man on a motorcycle offered
me a ride as I photographed the Forum;
a dozen teenage boys followed me
through the Tivoli Gardens, calling
"Come with us!"; and at a hotel bar
in Paris, an older man in a sagging
gray suit asked for my room number.
I said no, but he called later, said
he'd overheard it. Could he come up?

Now I can walk all the way around
Lucca on the Renaissance wall,
and no one looks twice: not the old
men with their wives, the young ones
eyeing girls in tights and short skirts,
the kids on bicycles, or the woman
with the little black dog. I am free
to sit on a bench and read. Fall leaves
glitter and spin above me while men
stop to say *"Buon giorno"* to the dog.

Sleeping in the Ruins

A hotel room in Lucca
      painted to resemble
            Roman ruins: crumbling
                  stone walls, moss and ferns
            sprouting in cracks

A real marble fireplace
      blends into the scene
            A trompe l'oeil frame
      hangs above the mantel

Breaks in the walls
      reveal olive trees
            and mountains, a domed
      pavilion with columns
            in the distance, everything
                  except sky and leaves
            in shades of white, gray and beige

An oriole perches
      on a decaying beam
            traversing the ceiling's blue sky
      dusted with clouds

White chrysanthemums
            bloom on the broken
                  terrace painted by the bed
where we wake
            to the rubble and small
                pulse of our lives
            and begin the task
                of saving what remains

Falling in Florence

I fell in the fall in Florence.
I've also fallen in New York,
Washington, DC, and Oakland,
California. My father and
grandmother had myasthenia
gravis, a disease that causes
muscle weakening and makes
one fall, but I don't think
I have it. Optimism? Denial?
I'm just a clumsy woman,
failing to look where I'm going,
and therefore fell on Via Cavour
in Florence after sharing a quatro
stagione pizza with my husband
at a café on Piazza San Marco
as I was thinking of the *Mocking
of Christ*, a fresco painted by Fra
Angelico in a monastery cell.
It's surreal, though created
in the fifteenth century: Christ,
blindfolded, is surrounded
by four disembodied hands
on a green background. One
holds a stick. There's also
a disembodied male head
in a hat, blowing something
on Christ's face. *Is it water
or spit or words of contempt?*
I wondered. Then I fell.

Climbing the Leaning Tower

Waiting in line, I'm giddy as a teenager.
Decades ago, I feared to go up.
Now, eager as the line starts moving,
I step briskly toward the tower, climb
the winding, tilted stairs with no railing,
just cracked stone walls on either side.

On the fourth floor and the seventh,
I go out to check the view, then keep
climbing, past the seven brass bells,
all the way to the top. The final flight
of stairs is narrow, has indentations
in the marble from centuries of feet.

High above red-tiled roofs, higher
even than the domes of the baptistry
and cathedral, I look at the hills
on the horizon, hunched under clouds.
What did I fear? That I would fall?
That someone would push me?

That the tower would finally topple
after more than six hundred years?
I start back down, thinking of what
I've missed: the lava flow on Kilauea,
pink dolphins of the Amazon, zip-lining
in Limón, the life I could begin today.

Flood in Venice

The hotel clerk handed us ugly boots
that came to our knees before
we went outside

where green water
from the canals poured
over the streets.

It was high tide and raining,
a routine flood.
By afternoon the water would recede,

leaving behind plastic bags and scraps
of soggy cardboard,
but as I slogged

through narrow streets, looking
in shop windows
for Murano glass jewelry,

I thought of Hurricane Katrina, the bloated
bodies in New Orleans,
and the earthquake that hit

Indonesia, how the sea was sucked out
all the way to the horizon,
then rose one hundred feet

and rushed forward
with biblical force.
I knew the sun would be back

the next day in Venice
to do its sparkly dance
around the gondolas, but as I paid

for necklaces with multicolored beads
shimmering like foil, I thought
of Noah and the *Titanic*—

water
as a wild card a jaded god
was holding—and might play.

II

Between the Two Shining Seas

Names of the States

Alabama, for the Alibamu tribe, forced from Alabama to Texas
when white people claimed their land in 1805

Alaska, for the Aleut word *alyeska*, meaning mainland, the place
toward which the sea flows

Arizona, the word for "small spring" in the O'odham language
of a Southwest desert people who couldn't vote until 1948

Arkansas, another name for the Quapaws, the Downsteam People,
who were removed to Oklahoma from their ancestral lands

Connecticut, from the Algonquian word for "long river place"

Delaware, from Baron De La Warr, Virginia's first governor,
whose name rechristened the local Lenni Lenape, the first tribe
to sign a treaty with the US

Hawaii, for "Hawai'iloa," discoverer of the islands
in Polynesian myth

Idaho, maybe Shoshone for "the sun comes down the mountain,"
or the Apache name for the Comanches, who drove them
from the southern Plains

Illinois, a French transliteration of *ilinwe*, the Ojibwe word
for the Inoka, whose thirteen tribes were reduced to five
by European disease

Indiana, Land of the Indians—the Delaware, Piankashaw,
Kickapoo, Wea, Shawnee, Miami, and Potawatomi—who were
mostly removed by 1846

Iowa, from the Dakota name for the Ioway tribe, meaning "sleepy ones"

Kansas, the Dakota word for the South Wind People, whose last fluent speaker of the Kansa language died in 1983

Kentucky, derived from the Iroquoian word for "on the meadow"

Massachusetts, People of the Great Hills—that is, the Blue Hills south of Boston Harbor—who were decimated by smallpox in 1633

Michigan, from *mishigamaa*, "great water," in the language of the Ojibwe, who like so many others, didn't understand the treaties ceding their land

Minnesota, from *mni sota*, the name the Dakotas gave the Minnesota River, whose clear blue water reflected clouds

Mississippi, from *misi-zibi*, Ojibwe for the "great river," along which more than twenty tribes lived and fished

Missouri, for the Missouria tribe that lived on the Missouri River, a Siouan people whose name means "town of the big canoes"

Nebraska, from *nebrathka*, the Omaha word for "broad water," a description of the Platte River, by which the tribe lived

New Mexico, named for the Mexicas, a Nahuatl-speaking people who ruled the Aztec Empire until the Spanish conquered them in 1519

North and South Dakota, named for a Sioux tribe whose men were sentenced in 1862 to the largest mass execution in US history, though Dakota means "friend"

Ohio, from *ohi:yo'*, "continuously giving river" in the language
of the Senecas, whose land was flooded in 1965, following
construction of Kinzua Dam

Oklahoma, from *okla humma*, Choctaw for "red people,"
a name proposed by the chief of the Choctaw Nation
during treaty negotiations in 1866

Oregon, maybe from *wauregan*, an Algonquian word
for "beautiful river," but so many Native words and languages
have been lost that it's hard to say

Tennessee, for the Cherokee town Tenasi, a village
on the Little Tennessee River until the Cherokees were marched
to Oklahoma along the Trail of Tears

Texas, meaning "friends" or "allies" in the language of the Caddos,
who were removed to Oklahoma in 1859

Utah, from *yuttahih*, an Apache word meaning "people
of the mountains"

Wisconsin, from *meskonsing*, the name for the Wisconsin River
in the Miami language: "river running through a red place"

Wyoming, a contraction of *mecheweamiing*, a Delaware word
first used for a valley in Pennsylvania, meaning "at the big plains"

And yes, every part of this land is Indian country, from forest
to desert, mountain to prairie, Manhattan to Yosemite,
Tallahassee to Seattle—all the fields, rivers, hills and canyons
between the two shining seas

Shoe Story

My sole started flapping like a huge
tongue on my left sneaker when I was
three thousand miles from home.

It was raining on Cape Cod
that summer day, and I'd brought
no other shoes except sandals.

I was afraid I might lose my sole or
it might trip me. The way it folded
back as I walked was truly scary.

So I bought new sneakers, pretty
black-and-white ones with mesh tops
and white soles to keep my feet dry

in the rain, but rain leaked through
the mesh and the fabric beneath it,
saturating my socks and feet.

The next day I bought waterproof
sneakers—green-and-brown ones—
so now I have four new soles.

This is the sole life I know where
you can throw out a worn-out sole
and get two or even four new ones,

then walk along the salt marsh as swans
glide in pooling light where Pilgrims first
met Wampanoags who used cordgrass

from the marsh for baskets, wore
deerskin *moccasinash*, and didn't need
these newcomers to save their souls.

On Nantucket

Near houses with gray shingles and white trim,
lined up on bluffs that overlook the sea,
monarchs and swallowtails dip and skim
rose hips gleaming like orange berries.

The ocean, a turquoise taffeta shawl,
falls on sand shoulders lit by a moon
radiant as a trillion-ton pearl
on a silken scarf of pink and maroon.

A fiery brooch, Aquarius glitters
while great blue whales call to their mates
in a pitch that you and I can't hear.
Then wind picks up and dune grass quivers
as we head inside and wrens migrate
to a place where sun swaddles the earth all year.

The Day We Missed Our Plane

Grass rippled greenly on the bluff
all the way to the wild roses. American
goldfinches flitted from tree to tree
in their black-and-yellow finery. A female
cardinal, crested and dusky red, hopped
on a table just outside the window,
and sunlight gleamed like tiny fires
on the sea off Nantucket. The coffee
was rich and steaming, and we chatted
with our friends so long there was no time
to get change for the bus at the store
or walk to the bus stop, so we borrowed
four dollars and Wade drove us to the bus,
parking to block it until we got on.
When we got off, we bought sandwiches
to have on the plane and a toy lobster
for four-year-old Autumn. Early for
the ferry, we waited in the shade
while the July sun hugged our luggage
as it held our place in line. The sea,
calm and blue-green, rocked us gently
all the way to Hyannis, where we picked
up our rental car and set off to get
a toy lobster for six-year-old Sabine,
who wanted one that said Cape Cod.
After several wrong turns we found
a gift shop with Cape Cod lobsters,
but they were bigger than the one
from Nantucket, so we bought two,
one for Autumn and one for Sabine,
and wondered what to do with the little one.

It was hot and there was a cool restaurant
on the same block as the gift shop,
and we were hungry, so we went in
and ordered chef's salads. Afterward
we got gas and set the GPS for Boston.
When we reached Highway 6, cars were
inching along like sea turtles over dunes
for as far as we could see. We looked
at each other and at the dome of sky,
so relentlessly blue. It was way
too late to fix this: we had goofed.

Behind the Scenes at the Museum
St. Paul, Minnesota

A science museum, big as a factory,
as much underground as above:
wide, white basement hallways,
fabrication rooms, stored collections.
A giant door leads to a gallery
of room-size vaults where temperature,
humidity and light are controlled.

In one, shelves hold jars of creatures
floating in fixative (shrimp,
crabs, mice, fetal mountain goats);
another has drawers of insects
(a huge butterfly with blue, iridescent
wings, a stick bug one foot long
from South America).

A whole vault for dinosaur bones,
another where a bison skeleton
has been assembled, then blessed
by tribal elders. More treasures:
a fossil tortoise, 350,000 years old;
a bald eagle, its white tail
and brown wings spread in a drawer.

Earrings of shiny green beetle wings
and a necklace of small birds
from Peru. From the Plains,
beaded moccasins and dresses.
Samples of corn: miniature ears,
red or brown, more than one hundred
years old, more nutritious and tasty

the curator says, than corn today.
Some corn now exists only here,
but the museum is planting seeds
to give the corn back to the tribes
who gave it to early anthropologists,
who couldn't give them back their land
but at least thought to save the sacred corn.

What Flows Into the Gulf of Mexico

Melted snow from the crests of the Rockies rushes
past pinyon pines   limber pines   lodgepole pines
corkbark firs   ponderosas   gathering silt as it reaches
bur oaks   cottonwoods   staghorn sumacs   silver maples
passes prairie cord grass   winds through cattails   duckweed
skunk cabbage   finally to mingle in the Mississippi
with water draining from thirty-one states where hunter-gatherers
lived with bison herds for ten thousand years

Now the river carries oven cleaner
human feces and caffeine
medical residue from hospitals and laboratories
scouring powder and soap from millions of houses
antibiotics from all the cattle ranches in the Midwest
solvents from farm-machinery plants
pesticides from corn and soybean fields
ingredients used to make plastic
enough estrogen from birth control pills to bend the genders of fish
thousands of tons of herbicides
fertilizers that cause algae to form massive green carpets in the gulf
which leads to an explosion of bacteria
that decompose algae and kill
everything in an area the size of Massachusetts each year

All this even *before* 206 million gallons of oil
from the Deepwater Horizon blowout
before hundreds of thousands of gallons of oil dispersant
containing chemicals that destroy red blood cells and cause cancer
It all enters the shimmering, translucent bodies
of arrow worms and dinoflagellates consumed by oysters
the algae scooped up and eaten by shrimp

the crabs that crush mollusks and shrimp with their chelipeds
the sea bass whose stout jaws clamp down on any smaller creature
Of course, it's in our blood and hair and fingernails
It floats in our hearts and permeates our brains as surely
as hope or anger   It's in your body and mine—
these molecules that cling like lovers to our bones

Red Rock Canyon

Low shrubs, creosote and blackbrush,
grayish, close to the ground as stones.
Yucca with fans of spiky leaves.
Junipers with blue berries and brownish
yellow clusters of mistletoe. Prints
on a rock: five Paiute hands, a thousand
years old. Scorpions five inches long.
All this in the desert fifteen miles west
of the Las Vegas Strip with its replicas
of the Eiffel Tower, the Rialto Bridge
and the Roman Forum, and all the
bells, lights and whistles of the casinos.
But even the forty-million-dollar
fountains with twelve hundred jets
shooting water five hundred feet
into the air, choreographed to music,
don't excite me as much as
Joshua trees, twisted and gnarled
into odd shapes, and broad vistas
where mountains striped red, yellow
and tan reach toward the sun.

Thinking of Barbara Rogers' Paintings During the Storm

When wind began to whistle and moan
at the almost empty Tucson airport
and all the lights went out,
then flickered as automatic doors
opened and closed repeatedly,
letting hail the size of walnuts
fly in and land on the carpet,
and thunder rumbled so loud
and near that the building
seemed to rattle and shake
while implacable rain fell
like waterfalls pounding
the roof, I thought of Barbara
who'd gone to Kauai
to paint tropical gardens
when a hurricane hit and waves
crashed over the house,
fragmenting shells and leaves,
blossoms, stones and moons
forever after in her paintings
so that all the dazzling elements
and colors seem to float
in water or rise in air,
and when I went to the counter
to check in for my flight
as computers rebooted
and lightning flashed,
rain shimmering on all
the windows, I wondered
if my flight would be cancelled

and if I too would find
something lush and delicate
I'd never dared imagine—
tattered jasmine and ferns,
spiny forms, dangerous
orchids adrift in the storm.

Flying West

The sunset flares rose, orange
and gold above a sea of fog
streaming in from the Pacific.

We pass over clouds tinged
pink like cotton balls
stained with nail polish.

The clouds, small at first
and far below us, grow larger
as we descend toward SFO.

In my window seat, I mention
none of this to the man
beside me, his head bowed.

He wears dark glasses. His
black jacket says "Blind Boys
of Alabama" on front and back.

I've heard them on YouTube,
singing "People Get Ready,"
but I cannot hear the music

I think must be playing now
in his head. So much beauty
unshared, so much unsaid.

Window Seat

The passing world beneath a plane is small—
each house a kernel from an ear of corn,
each sailboat a miniscule thorn—
like moments of the life you now recall.

The bay's a carpet strewn with whitecap lint,
and oaks are broccoli on knee-high mounds
where passion's conflagration has burned down
to a match's evanescent glint.

The valley's just a checkerboard of farms
in inky shadows made by popcorn clouds,
and all the trophies that once made you proud
have shriveled to a bunch of munchkin charms.

You see it all at once from far away:
the little things that mattered yesterday.

Oasis

At an oasis deep
in my left temporal lobe,
I encounter my soul
just before it leaves the party
at 33,000 feet where
the dead do as they please
and time is a circular target.

Where does meaning
lurk in a universe
where mountains are mangy
from fires and logging,
the President brags about
forcing himself on women,
and marksmen take aim?

In the heart of a hummingbird
beating more than one
thousand times each minute
during a rapid dive
in a high-speed chase,
while outside a bright theater
night ripens like an avocado
and a gunman decides
not to shoot after all
because consciousness
is a moth that finally got in.

At the Berkeley Rose Garden

A stone path shows the way
to a wooden bridge shaded
by two young spruces.
A creek splashes over a waterfall,
then purls below the bridge.

On the railing, generations
of lovers have carved their
names and intitials: Kat and Reg,
RH and DP, MO loves LR.

A breeze brings the scent
of Sweet Afton, Lucky Lady,
Gold Medal, Amber Cream,
Picasso and Shining Flare.
They wait in silks and armor.

Some have numerous small petals
like chrysanthemums,
others fewer, broader ones
that open to reveal anthers
dotted with black or red.

I will follow the stones
away from the bridge to touch
the corollas and give myself over
to the mindlessness of roses—
their perfumes, scarlets, golds
and electric jolts of pink.

Corpse Flower

Berkeley Botanical Garden, 2015

Day 1: Saturday

What an unfortunate name
for the world's largest flower!
But Trudy is what they call
the one at the Botanical Garden
where the parking lot is reserved
for guests of today's three
weddings. It's my lucky day:
at the back of the lot I find
a lone unreserved space,
pay my admission, and head
for the greenhouse to see
Trudy, whose scientific name,
Amorphophallus titanum,
means "titanic, misshapen
phallus." Green and wrinkly,
eight feet tall, this organ
is demurely enfolded
in a pleated green skirt
that should open tomorrow.

Day 2: Sunday

Attendants shoo me away
from the parking lot,
where all the spaces are
reserved for more weddings.
I have to drive half a mile
up the hill and take a shuttle
back to the garden, wait
in line for half an hour
for my ticket, then another

hour and a half to reach
the greenhouse, because
so many people can't
make it to the rainforests
of Sumatra but want to see
this flower, which isn't
really a single flower
but an inflorescence with
many male and female
blossoms and a stalk
that stinks like rancid meat
to attract beetles and flies
that revel in pollen while
looking for dinner. Stalk
and skirt have turned yellow
and the skirt has opened,
revealing a maroon lining.
This happens only once
every seven to ten years:
the phallus heating up
to human body temperature
and giving off its stench of
rotting fish and sweaty socks,
the female flowers maturing
before male ones to prevent
self-pollination, the whole
process over and insects
departing after only twelve
hours. As stalk and skirt
begin to shrivel, the plant
goes back to storing energy
in its corm, an underground
stem, like people toiling
for years at their secret work
and hoping that something
stupendous—and strong as
elephant sex—will emerge.

At Fensalden Inn

Albion, California

In the Hawthorne Room, here
at the inn—once a Wells Fargo
stagecoach stop—Nathaniel, ancestor
of the innkeeper, looks to the left
in his portrait above the mantle
in a black bow tie, white collar
and jacket with two rows of buttons.
He has pensive blue eyes, dark
wavy hair. I'd call him handsome.

Wearing my scarlet sweater, I sit
at his desk and open a green book,
first edition of *The Marble Faun*.
He had doubts about the existence
of the "Gentle Reader," that soul
"appreciative of his success,
indulgent of his short-comings,
and, in all respects, closer
and kinder than a brother."

Outside, watercolor clouds
dissolve above the lashing sea
while black-tailed deer graze
on grass surrounding the feeder
where this morning a jay,
red-winged blackbird, and flock
of band-tailed pigeons gathered
to bicker and chat. Wind thunders
like the sea in the distance.

The fire snaps its yellow fingers.
There's a dark scar on the left
side of the desk, a white lace doily
under a lamp on the right. I remember
a line of quail, bobbing their heads
as they strutted down the road
this afternoon, and ponder
feather plumes and the reader
who is neither gentle nor a friend.

Watching the Grebes

Clear Lake, California

A taut blue sky is stretched above the lake,
which glitters like a rippling field of stars
in early sun. Two Western grebes take
a morning swim, but they don't go far
before they plunge. When they emerge, beaks
filled with weeds, they stand. It's time to dance!
Long necks held high, black crests and white cheeks
side by side, they glide as though on skis, advance
toward us. Standing on the balcony,
we see the shining wake they leave behind.
My love, I'd like to be as easy
as the grebes, who seem content to find
a dancing partner as the new day starts—
a dark-winged bird that knows the steps by heart.

At Lake Tahoe

Granite mountains, dense with white firs,
lodgepole pines and ponderosas, rise abruptly
from the lake's blue bowl, so deep its waters
could cover all of California and Nevada.

The Washoes who lived here ten thousand summers
named it Lake in the Sky because it reflected
clouds, sunset and stars. They caught Lahontan trout
in the lake, mountain whitefish in icy streams.

On the other side of the continent, my Wampanoag
ancestors were gathering cranberries, covering
their summer homes with cattail mats, baking clams,
drying corn and fishing for salmon off Cape Cod.

The Washoes used only fallen trees for homes
they would dismantle before leaving Lake in the Sky
each winter. In fall they gathered piñon pine nuts
to eat until spring. This was before white people came

and cut down the piñon pines to build their houses,
dynamited the mountains in search of silver
and gold, and claimed the fish. Now, a paddleboat
with three decks takes tourists on cruises of Lake Tahoe.

Yet in summer Washoes still do the Pine Nut Dance,
and Wampanoags do the Grass Dance to keep the world
in balance and remind us that the Earth is living, every
rock is sacred, and every tree and salmon has a soul.

Elephant Seals

Año Nuevo, California

What are they thinking, stretched out in the sun
like logs or so many gargantuan sausages?
It looks like an easy life—lounging in a puddle
or sleeping on the beach. But something's going on:
roaring and drumming. They're making a racket.

Loser males lumber toward alphas, rear up,
get bitten, lumber off. Lolling on sand, do they plan
the next fight? Nine of ten males never get laid
in a lifetime. Do the losers complain to each other?
Do females brag about hundred-pound pups?

Does anyone dream about dinner? They don't eat
for months in winter. Do they remember diving
two thousand feet under the sea, holding
their breath for up to two hours to hunt for fish
and eels? They're lucky if the fish are mercury-free,

if storm waves wash no pups from the beach,
if they grow fat enough for a chance at bigamy.

Hamsa

A gold filigree amulet shaped like a hand
with three straight fingers,
symmetrical pinky and thumb curved outward,
a turquoise bead staring from the palm.

I bought it decades ago
at the Arab Market in Jerusalem
from a man in long robes, whose store
was a tent with Persian carpets.
He refused to bargain, said
it was real gold, the price fair.

It's the hand of Fatima,
daughter of Mohammed, to Moslems,
the hand of the Virgin Mary
to Levantine Christians,
the hand of Miriam, sister of Moses, to Jews.

"Hamsa" is from *hamesh* and *khamsa*,
Hebrew and Arabic for five:
five fingers, Five Books of Moses,
Five Pillars of Islam.
It wards off the evil eye.

My last day in Israel, the market closing soon,
I fastened it on a chain around my neck
to take the luck home. But now
when I wear it, Homeland Security
stops me at airports. Agents pat my legs,
make me unpack my carry-on luggage,
run their fingers through my hair.

When I wore it to Disneyland,
my four grandchildren waiting
in line behind me, a guard
felt my tote bag, then asked me to empty it.
The suspicious object? My banana.
Oh, what can we do to save
this world where people fear
a necklace might blow up
Donald Duck, or bring down a plane?

What the NSA Knows

the names of all your Facebook friends
the rides you liked at Disneyland
who rode with you on Splash Mountain
and what necklace you were wearing

who sent you a link to her reading in Houston
who wants the name of your publicist
who was worried that she offended you
and who invited you for coffee this afternoon

who left you voicemail messages on Monday
before speaking with you on Tuesday
who gave you the best bid on Wednesday
and which Latino contractor texted you today

that you ordered Cetaphil Moisturizing Lotion
and Neutrogena Fragrance-Free Hand Cream
on Amazon along with *The Crafty Poet,*
Miss Emily and *Surprise-Inside Cakes*

that you don't log onto Twitter every day
but you've tweeted things like the "Wake Up
and Take Action on Climate Change" petition
and "Dung Beetles Navigate Using the Stars"

the NSA has whole buildings of computers
with teams of engineers and systems analysts
to track your search for furry slippers
and tell the President what size you buy

The Logic of Comets

Comet Halley, 1986

Beyond the lodgepole pines on Jackass Hill
on a moonless morning at four a.m.,
from my boyfriend's garage roof I spot
a fuzzy snowball sailing just above
the southern horizon, under prickly stars.
Even with my binoculars, I can't see the tail,
like a frozen waterfall or bridal veil.
"I can see it!" my lover says, but doesn't
pass me *his* binoculars. *I must buy better
binoculars*, I tell myself as a barn owl
swoops below us and my heart hardens.

Comet Hyakutake, 1996

It blooms in the north—a giant dandelion
in the sky above the Berkeley hills, watered
by the Big Dipper. I'm glad the universe
hasn't collapsed into a black hole, but even
with new binoculars and a new boyfriend,
I see no tail draped across the night
above headlights, streetlights and houses.
The other dinner guests join me outside.
Craning our necks, we try, like magicians,
to pull a white scarf from the sky.

Comet Hale-Bopp, 1997

The night the newspaper says is best
for viewing—the night of the 92 percent
lunar eclipse—I stand alone on wet grass

at the Berkeley Marina. Following the logic
of comets, it appears: the huge blue ion tail,
just above hills across the bay, pointing
away from the sun; the yellow dust tail,
thinner, curving slightly. On the other side
of the sky, a rust-colored cap perches
above a black-masked face near Mars.
I'm lucky tonight, while the moon is dark!

Last Day of Zoo Camp
Oakland Zoo

Children, in blue-and-gold
Zoo Camp tee shirts, gather
at picnic tables on a hilltop
shaded by pines. They have met
the boa with its reddish brown
camouflage pattern; baboons
with butts callused for comfort;
fruit bats, which cannot
echolocate but see better
than any other bat; sun bears
with orange necklaces of fur;
and turtles, whose favorite
color is red. The little train
has taken the campers past
wallabies, emus and kangaroos,
which cannot walk backward.
They have hidden treats
for chimpanzees, whose DNA
is ninety-eight point four
percent identical to their own,
and watched them eat, eager
as children finding candy.
Now the campers sing about
penguins, which can stay
underwater for twenty minutes;
hippos with four-foot-tall smiles;
and tigers with striped skin
beneath their striped fur.
Parents and grandparents
look on—remarkable mammals
with twenty-six bones in each

foot, a nose that can remember
fifty thousand scents, a brain
that's eighty percent water,
and a charge to save this planet
where they are outweighed
by termites, ten to one.

Similes by Devlin, Age Four

He says the new chandelier in my front hall
with its five wavy amber-colored shades,
each holding a candle-shaped bulb,
"looks like honey dripping from flowers."

And the sound of tires on pavement
on a spring afternoon, as we drive
up the hill to Lawrence Hall of Science,
"is like the sizzle of pancakes cooking."

When I'm on the phone with his mom,
discussing dinner plans and weather,
he wants to tell me something:
"I love you more than an infinity of houses."

I think about that: the most expensive
and important thing anyone owns.
What can I say? Stars are too distant,
flowers too small and fragile. Stumped,
I reply, "I love you that much too."

Beauty and the Boy

For Devlin at Point Reyes

As we drive to the beach, my grandson,
age five, strapped in his car seat in back,
tells my husband and me between bites
of a chocolate chip cookie that he hopes
to be a parent when he grows up.

He wants two children, a boy and a girl
he'll name Golden Spider and Red Spider
because he likes gold and red and spiders:
they're pretty. He doesn't want a job,
he says, because he doesn't like money.

But how will he buy food and clothes
for Golden Spider and Red Spider,
we ask. Won't he need money for that?
He sighs, brow furrowed. "If I have
to work," he concedes, "I'll be a doctor."

Later, at the Visitor Center gift shop,
he scorns the sticker books and storybooks
we offer. I want a *real* book he says
indignantly, heading for the field guides
and systematically opening each one.

His choice: a guide to California species
with birds, insects, spiders, fish, reptiles,
mammals and even plants. He swoons over
the mountain king snake with red, white
and black bands. "That one's my favorite."

Book in hand, he heads for the beach,
using a log to cross a shallow channel
where he'll scout for crabs that saunter
sideways with their flat and crusty glamour
that puts even crimson spiders to shame.

I Am Amazed

By the Arches Cluster, the most
crowded place in the Milky Way,
jam-packed with stars, 25,000
light-years from Earth in Sagittarius

By Earth, whirling through space,
the only planet known to have
free oxygen, liquid water, whales,
wallabies and redwood forests

By a single redwood tree, 350
feet tall and ten feet in diameter,
standing above the Pacific
since Herod was exiled to Gaul

By a single redwood needle, flat,
with two silvery bands on its
underside and inner machinery
endlessly churning out ATP

By a molecule of ATP, which
carries energy in all the cells
of people and trees, a currency
required for love and breathing

By two children, a boy and a girl,
playing under the tree, who spot
a speckled woodpecker with a red
patch on its head, tapping the bark,

igniting a blaze of amazement

Redwoods and Rain

I am redwoods and rain,
stomata like green lips opening
for a kiss on the underside of leaves,
a leopard leaping high as a house,
its fur glowing with black-gold roses.

I am untold generations of ancestors,
back to the ones who painted
with charcoal on the walls of caves
and hunted aurochs and mammoths
across vast, uncharted plains.

I'm also the grandchildren whose small
hands I hold, and the great-grandchildren
who might or might not be born.
My elements come from supernovae
blown light-years across space.

I am mostly water, an ocean
of matter and energy grown conscious.
The fate of the Earth is my domain.
I am slime mold and diatoms,
bluebirds and dolphins, daisies,
archaebacteria, redwoods and rain.

Old Man

For Bill

Old man, gaunt, with scraggly gray hair
and cancer of the spine, greeting me
from your deathbed, what binds us now is
the past—the night when you were seventeen
and I was drunk and you pulled me away
from the boys who would abuse me.

We locked ourselves in a bedroom and kissed.
You said you wouldn't hurt me, and didn't,
your hair thick and black on the pillow. There
was that, and the day we rented bicycles
on Stanyan Street and rode them through
Golden Gate Park, all the way to the sea,

and the day we drove through the mountains
and stopped to ski, which neither of us
had ever done before. Take my hand. Let's
remember the sun beating on slushy snow
and how you skied all the way down
the intermediate slope without falling.

I don't believe in your death or mine,
but in colors and sky, all the possibilities
reflected in your hazel eyes, which glittered
like emeralds the night we danced naked.

It Happens

Whether we believe in it or not,
cells shut down, one by one:
no more diffusion of oxygen across
the porous endothelial lining
of capillaries in the lungs,
no more nerve impulses leaping
from node to node along the myelin sheaths,
no more ATP used up pumping potassium
into every cell and sodium out.

My friend Bill lies still now, eyes shut,
a total power blackout in his body.
Five burly men in green shirts turned
his casket to face the sea, then used straps
to lower it into the ground. I threw
in dirt and red carnations.
Now the oval, spiny-toothed leaves
of a coast live oak flicker above
his raw brown patch of earth.

Farther up the hill, past the fountains
ringed with cypresses like long
green fingers pointing toward the sky,
the ashes of my parents and daughter
are buried in bronze urns. My name
waits, already carved on granite
although wind caresses my arms
and the fountains murmur. I listen
for the lost as clouds keep churning.

Pageant Bouquet

With my Ms. Senior Sacramento Pageant bouquet,
I stand at my mother, father and daughter's grave
at Mountain View Cemetery. Throughout
my childhood, my dad always said he'd like
to go to Atlantic City with me someday,
and of course Mom shared his dream,
but I became a bride at fourteen, a mother
the following year of another little girl
who envisioned becoming a beauty queen.
Now, decades later, I finally have a tiara,
scepter, sash and bouquet of pink carnations,
purple Mexican sage, and fuchsia
pompons and spider mums interspersed
with shiny lemon leaves and silvery
spiral eucalyptus. But the two people who
planted this fantasy in me, and the daughter
who never entered a pageant, lie beneath
this hill, where the grass is finally green
again after years of drought. I fill the cone-
shaped flower container at a faucet under
a line of pines. Even the fountains
are flowing again, the sky blue, the bay
gleaming in the distance as I drive the spike
at the bottom of the container into the earth
in front of the headstone and arrange
the flowers. Mom, Dad, Liana, it's more
about fighting ageism now than proving
my beauty. I see that our days are numbered,
our wins too few, but possibility still feels
real as the sunlight washing over this hill.
A small bird is trilling; the bouquet is for you.

Come Back

I want you to push
that noisy toy vacuum cleaner
that plays the repetitive jingle
I want you to push it
over and over
while I try to read

I want you to throw a tantrum
in a store when I refuse
to buy you candy
and while I'm bathing
I want you to pour
all my lotions and perfumes
into the center of my bed

I want you to kick the table
when you don't like
what I'm serving for dinner
I want you to tell me
the way I exercise
is stupid and no good

I want you to cut school
and come home drunk
at dinnertime
I want you to borrow
my clothes without asking
and then lose them

I want you to date a man
who will steal $100

from the purse on my bed
I want you to work
as a flight attendant
and leave the iron on
when you go on a four-day trip

I want you to ask for money
for clothes, a car, school,
a wedding, a house,
lessons for your children
I'll help with anything again

I'm sitting in the kitchen
the phone is on
the line isn't busy
you can call me collect
but this time
you have to live

Dream of the Moving Chair

The chair on the terrace
where I sit is white, hard,
the black sea beside me
lit by stars so near
they seem like fireflies.
The whole universe sings
"Unchained Melody."
I join in, singing at the top
of my lungs, *Time goes by
so slowly, and time can do
so much.* A young woman
with long legs and long hair
runs by, and my chair starts
to move. Following her
down dark streets, I want
to protect her. She runs
past a knot of dangerous-
looking men. As though
propelled by my thoughts,
my chair moves faster.
*I'll be coming home, wait
for me.* The woman, swift
and lean, wearing shorts,
runs down a leafy street
and enters a building,
like a hotel, at the end.
My chair stops at the door.
I go in. My daughter Liana
looks at me with surprise,
"You came back!"
she says. "I'm so glad."

*

Oh my love, my darling,
it's such *a long, lonely*
time these two years since
you died. I'm glad you're
pleased to see me. Your
children are doing well
although they miss you.
How long was it before you
understood I was a child
myself, just fifteen, when

you were born? How many
times did I leave you
with grandparents?
Did I never tell you
I'd always come back?

Three Omens

What does it mean if you are fifteen
and nine months pregnant
when you find your parakeet dead—
a clump of yellow feathers
still warm on the dining room floor?
My mother said it meant nothing. A few
days later my first daughter was born,
and my childhood ended.

What does it mean if you are twenty-six,
nine months pregnant
for the second time, and find
a dead blackbird on an orange plate
on the kitchen table? My daughter
explained it had been wounded
and she brought it inside, hoping it would live.
A few days later my second daughter
was born, and my childbearing days ended.

What does it mean if you are sixty-six
and your husband says
there's a dead bird by the front door?
Lying on its back, it's a sparrow
with a white speckled breast,
its legs in the air like little
brown twigs. Perhaps it flew
against the window between
the porch and deck. I wonder:
What is beginning now?
What is coming to an end?

Toys in My House

On the stereo cabinet in the living room,
a black metal steam engine
my grandfather—who came to California
from Paterson, New Jersey, by train—
played with in the 1880s, when
women wore bustles and every year
more and more tracks were laid

Eighty-four glass marbles
in multicolored swirling shades
in a handmade beige cotton sack
on which my dad neatly
printed his initials, R.A.L.,
before the stock market crash,
when the Charleston was the rage

Perched on a closet shelf,
the Keystone Televiewer I used
to see naked children in 3D
outside their treelike huts
in the Belgian Congo, back
when blonds were called dumb
and people still did the jitterbug

The Candy Land game whose
plastic gingerbread people
my daughter Liana pushed
through the Lollypop Woods
when Tricky Dick was President
and hippies danced to the Dead,
high on mushrooms or weed

A doll, once Swan Lake Barbie
with long blond tresses, but who
got tattoos and short, spiky hair—
purple, pink and green—thanks
to my daughter Tamarind,
when Pac-Man was new
and Michael Jackson ruled MTV

Buzz Lightyear, waiting
for someone new to come along,
flip up his helmet and hear him say,
"To infinity and beyond!" now
that my grandson Brandon,
almost twelve, would rather play
Jetpack Joyride on his iPod

The miniature horse ranch set
with white, chestnut, gray
and tan steeds whose jockeys
ride them over hurdles in
the hands of my granddaughters,
Autumn and Sabine, who still
are masters of make-believe

.

A plastic car that plays
the Mickey Mouse Club Song
for Devlin, my younger
grandson, who scoots
around the living room, unaware
that the world will change,
just glad to toot the horn today

Downwind from the Flames

Feathery branches of the redwood in my backyard
hang motionless. I haven't heard
a single birdcall in today's unrelenting haze.

The fire is two hundred miles away in a town
called Paradise; heaven and hell
got mixed up and now occupy one space.

Even at this distance, we're told to stay indoors,
air cleaners on, windows closed.
Outdoors, everything dissolves in toxic fog.

I've seen a conflagration up close: the hills
of my own city topped with flames,
incinerating trees and houses in their way.

They burned fast and furious as youthful passion,
devouring oxygen I meant to breathe.
Only fireplaces and chimneys were left standing.

In other people's yards, I mourned amid ashes
and potsherds, but my own house
remained intact while my life blazed away.

After Catastrophe

Go to sleep. You need your dreams
as much as ever. Maybe more.
When you wake, make yourself a cup
of coffee, Conscientious Objector,
Certified Fair Trade and Organic,
a blend of Guatemalan, Ethiopian
and Sumatran beans. Do not
avoid the newspaper: no matter
how upsetting, you need to know
what's going on. Remember that
the redwood tree is still alive
even though it has fungal cankers
and you must keep pruning away
infected branches. So too with
society, which suffers from fear
and hatred, ancient diseases
that must continually be cut away.
Give the plants on your deck
some water. The geranium, fuchsia
and impatiens are still blooming
even though it's nearly winter.
Find solace in their resilience.
Then take your grandchildren
to a movie, *The Eagle Huntress*,
to remind them and yourself
that the Earth is gorgeous, even
when cold and dangerous, that
societies can evolve and change,
allowing a young girl in Mongolia
to take on a role once filled only
by men. Think about that girl

with an eagle perched on her arm
and ask yourself what you can do
to ensure that spring will come
again, with all the stars in place.

Trespasser

The man who lived under my garage
broke into the storage space, replaced
my lock with his own to doze beside
the woodpile in an orange sleeping bag
with a blue sheet, his head resting
on a dirty pillow. He ate saltines,
drank beer, and read *The Scarecrow, Mercy,*
Hell's Corner, The Scarpetta Factor
and *The Magick of Sex.* When he rose
he put on black boots, cracked and crusty,
and a tattered backpack to sell
Street Spirit and panhandle near Safeway.

I changed the lock and left his things outside
in four large trash bags and two crates
with notes asking him to take them away.
Of course, he never did. But he came back,
easily picked the lock to my dreams
to drift past rocky islands in a red canoe
with no paddles, his shattered reflection
wavering on green water, and stand
beneath a giant poison mushroom
for protection from rain as I worried
where he slept now and watched him
step from the black-and-white world
of an old film into rainbow flames.

Mosquitoes

I've been bitten in six countries
on three continents.
They swarm around me
and bite through my clothes,
leaving welts two inches in diameter.

It's happened as I ate a hamburger
at a barbecue in Massachusetts,
lay by a pool in Costa Rica,
watched a toucan in Ecuador,
browsed in a gift shop in Athens,
admired flamingoes and white horses
in the Camargue of southern France.

My first time in Mexico, dining
outdoors in Puerto Escondido, I got
72 bites from *Anopheles* before
I could even seize the insect repellent.

Females are the mean ones,
with their long probosces that pierce
your skin to suck your blood,
at the same time injecting malaria,
yellow fever, chikungunya, dengue fever,
philariasis, West Nile or Zika virus.
Earth's deadliest animals, they kill
more than 700,000 people each year.

Twenty percent of people
are especially delicious, and I am
one of them, a mosquito magnet

with Type O blood, excreting lactic
acid and exhaling CO_2 detected
by the lady mosquitoes' maxillary palps.

I am tired of wearing long sleeves
in tropical countries, slathering
myself with repellent, or staying indoors.
No way am I going to India or Africa.
Look for me next on a glacier in Iceland,
perhaps glimpsing a reindeer,
or maybe in Antarctica, surrounded
by penguins waddling around
in tuxedos, without any shoes.

Going

I always used to think I was going somewhere:
to work at the little health museum under the movie theater
to a meeting with my boss at the hospital on the other side of town
to Paris where I could have an affair with a handsome Frenchman
to New York where I might find an agent to sell my book
to a romantic restaurant for dinner with my husband

to the movie
where a serviceman falls in love
to the movie
where a married couple is always fighting
to the movie
where an old couple looks backward and forward
wondering if they're still in love

back to my house, which is always in need of paint or repairs

to a better job
a better vacation
a better house
a better marriage
a better movie
a better life

Now I see all destinations as steppingstones—
just temporary stops until the last
the journey itself as a sack of diamonds
all journeys as one journey
with wind or wheels propelling me forward
through desert and forest as I create the only path

Acknowledgments

I am grateful to my husband, Richard Michael Levine, and to my many poet friends—including Susan Gubernat, Nellie Hill, and Naomi Ruth Lowinsky—for helping me improve these poems. Susan Terris deserves a special thanks for her insights both on individual poems and on the manuscript as a whole. I also wish to thank Marcia Falk, whose poems and beautiful books have inspired me for many years. The poem "I Am Amazed," p. 91, is dedicated to Susan Duhan Felix, ceramic artist and beloved Art Ambassador for the City of Berkeley, who signs her correspondence "Stay amazed."

The lovely design by Melanie Gendron and the support of Diane Frank, chief editor of Blue Light Press, have been crucial to bringing this book into the world. Finally, I am indebted to the editors of the following publications, in which many of the poems have appeared, sometimes in slightly different form:

Ambush Review: "What Flows Into the Gulf of Mexico"

America, We Call Your Name (Sixteen Rivers Press): "Inauguration Day in the Galápagos"

Assisi: An Online Journal of Arts & Letters: "At the Berkeley Rose Garden," "Child's Grave and Finery," "Redwoods and Rain," "Similes by Devlin, Age Four," "Toys in My House"

Atlanta Review: "The Real Thing"

Arroyo Literary Review: "Clichés from the Caves," "Falling in Florence"

Blue Unicorn: "Yom Kippur in Ephesus and Patmos"

California Quarterly: "*Buon Giorno*," "Downwind from the Flames," "Reverie Interrupted," "Roses," "TGV, Paris to Arles"

Canary: A Literary Journal of the Environmental Crisis: "Last Day of Zoo Camp," "What the Tortoises Know"

The Color of Being Born (Jaded Ibis Press): "Watching the Grebes"

The Crazy Child Scribbler: "Hologram"

decomP magazinE: "Three Omens"

FRiGGmagazine.com: "Climbing the Leaning Tower," "Thinking of Barbara Rogers' Paintings During the Storm"

Ekphrasis: "Pygmalion"

The Gathering 12: "Window Seat"

The Green Door: "Empire of Lights," "Water Lilies"

Hawai'i Pacific Review: "Old Man"

The Hudson Review: "At Fensalden Inn"

Iodine Poetry Journal: "The Lark's Wing, Encircled with Golden Blue, Rejoins the Heart of the Poppy Sleeping on the Diamond-Studded Meadow"

Know Me Here: An Anthology of Poetry by Women (WordTemple Press): "After Catastrophe"

LevureLittéraire.com: "Resplendent Quetzels"

Lips: "Last Day in Amsterdam"

Marin Poetry Center Anthology: "Artists at Chauvet," "Flood in Venice," "Fountain," "Time on Rábida"

Marsh Hawk Review: "Dining Alone in Athens"

Naugatuck River Review: "Dinner in Barcelona," "Dream of the Moving Chair"

Nimrod International Journal: "It Matters"

North Coast Literary Review: "On Nantucket"

Paterson Literary Review: "Foreigner"

Pinyon Commemorative Issue: "Abandoned in Sarlat," "Hamsa"

Pleiades: "Come Back"

Poetry Expressed Magazine: "Flying West"

PoetryMagazine.com: "The Logic of Comets"

Psychological Perspectives: "Beauty and the Boy," "Corpse Flower," "Evenk Shaman's Costume," I Am Amazed," "It Happens," "Red Rock Canyon"

Red Indian Road West: Native American Poetry from California (Scarlet Tanager Books): "At Lake Tahoe" *riverbabble*: "Almost Mugged in Lucca," "Global Warming in the Galápagos"

The San Francisco Chronicle: "Pageant Bouquet"

San Francisco Peace and Hope: "Going"

Talking Writing: "Birthday Gifts from the Rain Forest," "Elephant Seals," "Oasis," "What the NSA Knows"

Tule Review: "Fiesta," "Sleeping in the Ruins"

U.S. 1 Worksheets: "Vincent's Bedroom in Arles"

Valparaiso Poetry Review: "Birds of San Pancho"

Yellow Medicine Review: "Names of the States"

ZYZZYVA: "Trespasser"

The following poems were nominated for a Pushcart Prize: "Falling in Florence" by *Arroyo Literary Review*, and "Names of the States" by *Yellow Medicine Review*. "Fiesta" was reprinted in *The Gathering 14*, "The Logic of Comets" in *Celestial Musings: Poems Inspired by the Night Sky*.

The chapbook *Dreaming of Sunflowers: Museum Poems* (Blue Light Press), recipient of the 2014 Blue Light Poetry Prize, included these poems: "Artists at Chauvet," "Behind the Scenes at the Museum," "Clichés from the Caves," "The Empire of Lights," "Evenk Shaman's Costume," "Falling in Florence," "The Lark's Wing, Encircled with Golden Blue, Rejoins the Heart of the Poppy Sleeping on the Diamond-Studded Meadow," "Last Day in Amsterdam," "Pygmalion," "Sleeping in the Ruins," "Vincent's Bedroom in Arles," "Water Lilies."

About the Author

Lucille Lang Day has published six previous full-length poetry collections, including *Becoming an Ancestor*, and four chapbooks, including *Dreaming of Sunflowers: Museum Poems*. She is also a coeditor of two anthologies, *Red Indian Road West: Native American Poetry from California* and *Fire and Rain: Ecopoetry of California*, and the author of two children's books, *Chain Letter* and *The Rainbow Zoo*, and a memoir, *Married at Fourteen: A True Story*, which was a finalist for the Northern California Book Award in Creative Nonfiction. Her books have received the Joseph Henry Jackson Award in Literature, the Blue Light Poetry Prize, and two PEN Oakland/ Josephine Miles Literary Awards; her poems, short stories, and essays have received ten Pushcart Prize nominations and have appeared widely in magazines and anthologies. The founder and director of Scarlet Tanager Books, she received her MA in English and MFA in creative writing at San Francisco State University, and her BA in biological sciences, MA in zoology, and PhD in science/mathematics education at the University of California, Berkeley.
http://lucillelangday.com

CPSIA information can be obtained
at www.ICGtesting.com
Printed in the USA
FSHW021939210720